# Ben Richards

I0149941

# Shadows of the Moon

A Collaboration by the young students that attend Pittman Recreation Center

3G Publishing, Inc.
Loganville, Ga 30052
www.3gpublishinginc.com
Phone: 1-888-442-9637

First published by 3G Publishing, Inc. September, 2024.

ISBN: 978-1-941247-60-0

Printed in the United States of America

# Ben Richards - New Beginnings

In the cozy town of Willowbrook, where the streets were lined with colorful houses and the air smelled of freshly baked cookies, there lived a boy named Ben Richards. Ben was just like any other kid his age, playful, adventurous, and always up for a good time. But Ben had a secret, one that he couldn't quite explain.

Ben's best friend was Sebastian, a boy who lived in a grand mansion on the outskirts of town. Sebastian's family had more money than they knew what to do with, but despite their differences, Ben and Sebastian got along like two peas in a pod. Along with their friends Alexis, Alex, and Mia, they formed a tight-knit group known as the Willowbrook Gang.

But even amidst all the laughter and fun, Ben couldn't shake the feeling that something was missing. You see, Ben was adopted by Amy and George, two of the most loving parents a kid could ask for. They treated Ben like their own flesh and blood, but deep down, Ben couldn't help but wonder about his real parents.

As Ben's 14th birthday approached, he felt a strange tingling sensation in his bones, like something was about to change. Unable to contain his excitement, Ben confided in Sebastian and the gang, telling them about the strange dreams he'd been having and the peculiar feelings stirring inside him. The night of Ben's birthday was unlike any other. As the clock struck midnight, a strange energy filled the air, and Ben felt himself being pulled towards the moonlit woods on the outskirts of town. With a mixture of fear and excitement coursing through his veins, Ben set off into the unknown, his friends trailing behind him.

But as they ventured deeper into the woods, the night took a sinister turn. Shadows danced in the moonlight, and strange noises echoed through the trees. Before they knew it, Ben and his friends found themselves lost in the darkness, with no idea which way to turn.

As they stumbled through the underbrush, Ben felt a strange sensation wash over him – a tingling in his fingers, a tightening in his chest. And then, without warning, it happened. Ben's body contorted and twisted, his skin rippling as fur sprouted from every pore. In a matter of seconds, Ben had transformed into a creature straight out of a nightmare – a werewolf.

Terrified and confused, Ben's friends didn't know what to do. But before they could react, Ben bolted into the night, his senses heightened and his instincts screaming at him to run. And run he did, deep into the heart of the forest, where he stumbled upon an old chicken coop nestled amongst the trees.

Exhausted and disoriented, Ben collapsed inside the coop, his mind reeling from the chaos of the night. When he awoke the next morning, he found himself covered in feathers, with a strange taste in his mouth. It was then that Ben realized the truth – he wasn't just a boy anymore, he was something else entirely. And as he looked out at the world through eyes that glowed like molten gold, Ben knew that his life would never be the same again.

# Adventure 1: The Secret Library

The sun was shining and the air smelled of freshly baked cookies as usual. Ben Richards, along with his friends Sebastian, Alexis, Alex, and Mia, were spending the afternoon exploring Sebastian's grand mansion. They had spent countless days here, but today felt different, like there was an adventure waiting to happen.

While rummaging through the attic, Alexis called out, "Hey, look what I found!" She held up a dusty old map with strange markings on it. The gang gathered around her, curiosity sparkling in their eyes.

Sebastian's eyes widened as he examined the map. "This looks ancient! We have to find out where it leads." "Yeah, it could be our next big adventure!" Ben said, feeling the familiar tingle of excitement in his bones. They quickly packed their bags with snacks, flashlights, and a sense of adventure, ready to uncover the secrets hidden in the woods.

They followed the map's winding path, which led them deeper into the forest than they had ever been before. The journey was full of tricky puzzles and booby traps. At one point, they had to figure out how to cross a stream using only the stepping stones that didn't sink. Mia, with her quick thinking, spotted a pattern and led them across safely.

Further along, they encountered a wall of vines with thorny branches. Alex suggested they look for a hidden switch or mechanism. After a bit of searching, Ben found an old lever disguised as a tree branch. Pulling it revealed a hidden passageway through the vines.

Finally, they arrived at a massive, hollow tree. The tree's trunk was enormous, with a door carved into its side. The gang pushed it open and stepped inside, their flashlights cutting through the darkness. To their amazement, they found themselves in a secret library filled with ancient books and scrolls.

"Wow, look at all these books!" Mia exclaimed, her eyes wide with wonder. They spread out, examining the shelves. Sebastian found a book about mythical creatures, while Alexis discovered a section dedicated to werewolves. Ben's heart raced as he picked up a particularly old tome with a faded cover. Inside, he found detailed descriptions of werewolf lore and history, along with hints about his own condition.

"Guys, check this out," Ben said, showing them a page about a powerful artifact that could help control werewolf transformations. "This could be the key to understanding and controlling my abilities."

The gang gathered around, feeling a mix of excitement and determination. They knew this was just the beginning of their journey. With the information they had uncovered, they were ready for whatever challenges lay ahead.

As they left the library, the sun was setting, casting a golden glow through the trees. The Willowbrook Gang felt more connected than ever, knowing they were on the path to discovering the secrets of Ben's true identity.

"We did it," Ben said, smiling at his friends. "And this is just the start."

Together, they walked back to town, their hearts full of hope and excitement for the adventures to come.

# Adventure 2: The Moonlit Lake

The summer nights were filled with the scent of blooming flowers and the sound of crickets chirping. One such evening, the Willowbrook Gang was gathered in Mia's backyard, roasting marshmallows over a crackling fire. As the flames flickered, Mia's grandmother, known for her intriguing stories, decided to share a tale.

"Have you ever heard of the Moonlit Lake?" she began, her voice full of mystery. "It's said that on the night of a full moon, the lake glows with magical properties. Legends say it can help those seeking answers about their true nature."

Ben's ears perked up. "Do you think it could help me understand my werewolf abilities?" "It's worth a try," Mia said, her eyes sparkling with excitement. "The next full moon is just a few days away. We should go check it out."

The gang agreed, and the days leading up to the full moon were filled with preparation. They packed tents, sleeping bags, and plenty of snacks, ready for their nighttime expedition.

On the night of the full moon, they set off for the lake, their flashlights cutting through the darkness. As they ventured deeper into the woods, an eerie fog began to roll in, and strange animal sounds echoed around them.

"Stay close," Sebastian said, trying to keep the group together. The fog made it hard to see, but they pressed on, drawn by the allure of the legendary lake.

As they neared the lake, they noticed the plants around them glowing faintly, illuminating their path. It was both beautiful and slightly unsettling. Finally, they reached the shore and set up their camp, eager to witness the lake's supposed magic.

At midnight, the moon rose high in the sky, casting a silvery light over the water. To their amazement, the lake began to glow with an ethereal light, shimmering like liquid moonlight. Ancient runes appeared on the shore, glowing softly.

"Look at that!" Alex exclaimed, pointing to the runes. "It's just like the legend said."

Ben, feeling a pull towards the water, stepped closer. "I have to see what happens," he said, kneeling by the edge and reaching out to touch the glowing surface. The moment his fingers made contact, a vision overtook him.

In the vision, Ben found himself in a forest, facing an old werewolf with wise, golden eyes. "Who are you?" Ben asked, feeling both awe and curiosity.

"I am Aric, an ancient werewolf guardian," the figure replied. "You have much to learn about your abilities, young one. Control comes from understanding and accepting your true nature."

The vision shifted, showing Ben different techniques to manage his transformations, emphasizing calmness and focus. "Remember, your friends are your strength," Aric said, before the vision faded away.

Ben blinked, finding himself back by the lake, his friends

looking at him with concern. "Are you okay?" Mia asked, her hand on his shoulder.

Ben nodded, feeling a new sense of confidence. "I met an old werewolf named Aric. He showed me how to control my transformations better. I think I can manage it now, at least partially."

The gang cheered, relieved and excited by the news. They spent the rest of the night sharing stories and enjoying the magical glow of the lake, feeling more united than ever.

As dawn approached, they packed up their camp, heading back to Willowbrook with a renewed sense of purpose. Ben felt more in control and ready for whatever lay ahead, knowing he had his friends by his side.

"We did it," Ben said, smiling as they walked. "And I couldn't have done it without you all."

Together, they returned to town, their bond stronger and their spirits high, ready for the next adventure that awaited them.

# Adventure 3: The Underground Labyrinth

Willowbrook's the summer days were filled with sunshine and laughter. However, one afternoon, the Willowbrook Gang—Ben, Sebastian, Alexis, Alex, and Mia—found themselves in the dusty old library of Sebastian's grand mansion. Sebastian had stumbled upon an intriguing discovery: an old diary that belonged to his great-grandfather.

"Listen to this," Sebastian said, his eyes scanning the yellowed pages. "Great-grandfather wrote about an underground labyrinth hidden beneath Willowbrook. It supposedly houses an ancient werewolf relic."

Ben's heart skipped a beat. "A relic? Do you think it could help me understand my powers better?"

"It's worth a shot," Sebastian replied. "But we'll need to be prepared. The labyrinth sounds like it's full of challenges."

The gang spent the next few days gathering supplies—flashlights, ropes, maps, and plenty of snacks. They carefully planned their exploration, determined to navigate the labyrinth and find the relic.

Early one morning, they set off towards the hidden entrance described in the diary. The entryway was concealed in a dense thicket at the edge of town. With some effort, they cleared the brush and uncovered a trapdoor leading down into darkness.

"Here goes nothing," Alex said, as they descended into the underground labyrinth. Their flashlights pierced the inky blackness, revealing stone walls covered in moss and cob-webs.

The labyrinth was a maze of shifting walls, hidden traps, and confusing passageways. At one point, they encountered a room where the walls moved, threatening to trap them. Mia, with her quick reflexes, noticed a pattern in the movements and guided them safely through.

Next, they found themselves in a corridor lined with ancient runes. As they carefully made their way forward, Alexis deciphered the runes to deactivate a series of traps that would have released a torrent of water.

After what felt like hours of navigating the labyrinth's twists and turns, they finally reached the center—a grand chamber with a pedestal in the middle. On the pedestal sat an ancient relic, glowing with a soft, pulsing light.

"This must be it," Ben said, feeling a strange pull towards the relic. He reached out and touched it. Instantly, a surge of energy coursed through him, connecting him to his werewolf side in a way he had never felt before.

Visions flooded his mind—images of past werewolves, their powers, and how they controlled them. Ben felt a deep sense of understanding and control. When the visions faded, he looked at his friends, his eyes glowing with newfound confidence.

"I feel… different. Better," Ben said. "I think I understand my powers now."

The gang cheered, thrilled by their success. They knew that this journey had brought them closer, not just to the relic, but to each other. Their shared experience in the labyrinth had strengthened their bond and proved their courage.

As they made their way back out of the labyrinth, they felt a sense of accomplishment and excitement for the future. They knew that with each adventure, they were growing stronger and more united.

"Thanks, everyone," Ben said as they emerged into the day-light. "I couldn't have done this without you."

"We're in this together," Mia replied, smiling.

Together, they walked back to Willowbrook, ready to face whatever challenges lay ahead. They knew that as long as they had each other, they could overcome anything. The adventure in the underground labyrinth had not only helped Ben understand his powers but had also cemented their friendship, making them more like family than ever before.

# Adventure 4: The Haunted Mansion

Whispers of a haunted mansion on the outskirts had always been a favorite topic of ghost stories. One day, while browsing through the local library, Alex stumbled upon an old newspaper article that caught his eye.

"Guys, check this out," Alex said, gathering the gang around a dusty table. "This article talks about the old Willow Mansion. There have been werewolf sightings around it, and it mentions a scientist who used to live there and experiment on werewolves."
Ben's eyes widened. "Do you think we might find more answers about my transformation there?"

"Only one way to find out," Sebastian replied, grinning. "Let's spend the night at the mansion and see what we can uncover."

The gang prepared for their spooky adventure, packing flashlights, blankets, snacks, and a map of the mansion they found in the library. As night fell, they set off towards the mansion, their hearts pounding with a mix of fear and excitement.

The mansion loomed before them, its windows dark and its walls covered in ivy. As they pushed open the creaky front door, it let out a ghostly wail that sent shivers down their spines.

"This place gives me the creeps," Mia whispered, clinging to Alexis. "Stay close," Ben said, leading the way with his flashlight.

The gang bravely explored the mansion's spooky hallways and creaky floors. Shadows seemed to dance on the walls, and ghostly apparitions flickered in and out of sight. Despite the eerie atmosphere, they pressed on, determined to uncover the mansion's secrets.

In one room, they found a hidden passage behind a bookshelf, leading to a small library filled with old journals and documents. Alexis carefully opened one of the dusty journals and began to read aloud.

"This journal belonged to Dr. Erasmus, a scientist who lived here," Alexis said. "He experimented on werewolves, trying to understand their powers and transformations."

"Maybe his notes can help us understand your condition better, Ben," Sebastian suggested.

They continued their exploration, discovering more hidden rooms and eerie artifacts. In the basement, they stumbled upon Dr. Erasmus's old laboratory. The room was filled with strange equipment, vials of mysterious liquids, and piles of handwritten notes.

Ben carefully examined the notes, feeling a sense of connection to the long-departed scientist. "These notes are incredible. Dr. Erasmus documented everything about werewolf transformations. This could really help me."

The gang spent hours poring over the notes, learning about different techniques and theories. The more they read, the more they understood about Ben's condition and how to control it.

As dawn approached, they packed up the notes and made their way out of the mansion, feeling a sense of accomplishment and newfound knowledge.

"We did it," Ben said, smiling at his friends as they emerged into the early morning light. "I know so much more about my powers now."

"And we did it together," Alex added. "We can face anything as long as we stick together."

The gang walked back to Willowbrook, their hearts full of pride and their bond stronger than ever. They knew that no matter what challenges lay ahead, they could overcome them as a team. The haunted mansion had not only given them more insight into Ben's transformation but also reinforced their friendship and courage.

As they reached the town, the sun was rising, casting a golden glow over Willowbrook. The gang felt ready for whatever adventure came next, confident that they could face anything together.

# Adventure 5: The Search for Elora

The Willowbrook Gang—Ben, Sebastian, Alexis, Alex, and Mia—found themselves on their most exciting adventure yet. This time, they were in a foreign country, following clues that pointed to more about Ben's mysterious condition. The clues led them to a small, picturesque town nestled between lush green hills and a sparkling lake. Here, they hoped to uncover more about Ben's origins.

Their journey took an unexpected turn when they found themselves being pursued by a shadowy clan known as the Danashi. The Danashi were known for their fierce loyalty to ancient secrets and their determination to keep certain knowledge hidden. As Ben and his friends navigated the narrow streets of the town, they could feel the Danashi closing in.

Just when it seemed they had no escape, a mysterious figure appeared and intervened, helping them slip away. The gang followed their savior to a secluded spot by the lake, where she finally introduced herself.

"I'm Elora," she said, her eyes meeting Ben's. "I'm your cousin, and I have the same condition you do."

Ben's heart raced. "You're a werewolf too?" Elora nodded. "I've been living here, trying to stay hidden from the Danashi. They don't want our kind to discover our true potential."

The gang sat by the lake, sharing stories and learning from Elora about their shared heritage. She explained how their family had been protecting powerful secrets for generations, secrets that the Danashi desperately wanted to keep buried. As they talked, the sky began to darken, and Elora's expression grew serious. She stood up suddenly, her gaze fixed on the distant woods. "I have to go," she said urgently. "They're coming."

Before anyone could react, Elora sprinted into the woods. The gang watched, stunned, as she disappeared among the trees. Ben's heightened senses allowed him to hear her rapid footsteps, but then he heard something else—rustling and whispers, growing louder.

"We need to follow her," Ben said, determination in his voice. "She might need our help."

The gang gathered their belongings and dashed into the woods, following the sounds of Elora's retreat. As they ventured deeper, the forest grew denser, and the whispers became more distinct. Shadows moved in the underbrush, and the air felt charged with an eerie energy.

Suddenly, they stumbled upon a clearing where Elora stood facing a group of Danashi warriors. The clan members were closing in, their eyes gleaming with malicious intent. "We have to help her!" Mia whispered urgently.

Ben, feeling a surge of newfound confidence, stepped forward. "Leave her alone!" he shouted, drawing the attention of the Danashi.

Elora glanced back at them, relief washing over her face. "Ben, you and your friends need to get out of here!" "No," Ben replied firmly. "We're in this together."

The gang formed a protective circle around Elora, ready to defend her. The Danashi hesitated, surprised by the unity and bravery of the group. Just as a confrontation seemed inevitable, a deep, resonant howl echoed through the forest. The sound was powerful and commanding, causing the Danashi to freeze.

From the shadows emerged a massive wolf, its eyes glowing with a fierce intelligence. The presence of the creature was enough to send the Danashi retreating into the forest, their resolve shaken.

Elora sighed in relief, the tension draining from her body. "Thank you," she said, turning to the gang. "You saved me." "We're family," Ben said, smiling. "We stick together."

As they made their way back to the lake, the gang felt a deeper sense of connection and purpose. Elora shared more about their family history, explaining the importance of staying united against the Danashi.

By the time they reached the lake, the sun was beginning to rise, casting a golden light over the water. Elora looked at the horizon, a thoughtful expression on her face. "There's still so much to learn," she said softly. "But I know we can face it together." Ben nodded, feeling a renewed sense of hope. "We'll find the answers, and we'll protect our family's legacy."

The gang sat by the lake, the dawn light reflecting in their eyes. They knew that this adventure had brought them closer, not just as friends, but as a family united by destiny. With Elora by their side and the support of each other, they were ready to face whatever challenges lay ahead, confident in their bond and their strength.

# Adventure 6: The Search for Elora (Continued)

As the sun rose higher, casting a warm glow over the lake, Ben looked at his friends and then back at Elora. "We have to go home soon," he said reluctantly. "My parents need me back in Willowbrook."

Elora's face fell, and she looked at Ben with sadness in her eyes. "What? I thought you would stay here with me." Ben sighed, feeling a tug at his heart. "I'm only 14, Elora. My parents would worry. They need me back home."

Elora's expression turned to one of sorrow and frustration. "Fine, leave me like they left us." Ben was taken aback. "What do you mean? Don't you have a family?"

Elora's eyes glistened with unshed tears. "Yeah, you. You're my family." Sebastian stepped forward, trying to ease the tension. "Elora, why don't you come back with us? You don't have to stay here alone."

Ben, still puzzled, asked softly, "Who left us?" Elora quickly shook her head. "Nevermind. You guys go. I have things to finish out here. I'll be safe." She pulled them all into a tight hug, her embrace lingering a bit longer with Ben. As she did, she discreetly slipped a small note into Ben's pocket.

Ben and his friends felt a mix of emotions as they started their journey back to Willowbrook. They couldn't shake the feeling that there was more to Elora's story than she had let on.

Later, when they were back at their cozy campsite, Ben remembered the note. He pulled it out of his pocket and unfolded it. The note was written in a hurried script:

"Ben,

There's so much I didn't get to tell you. Our family is more connected to this place than you know. The Danashi are a real threat, and I've been trying to protect our heritage. Please be careful. If you ever need me, I'll be here.

Stay strong, Elora."

Ben read the note aloud to his friends, his voice wavering with emotion. "She's been dealing with this all on her own," he said quietly.

"We'll find a way to help her," Alexis said firmly. "We're not going to let her face this alone." "Absolutely," Mia added. "We're family, and family sticks together."

As they packed up their camp and prepared to head home, Ben felt a renewed sense of purpose. He knew that their adventures were far from over, and that one day, they would return to help Elora and uncover the full truth about their shared heritage.

For now, they had to return to Willowbrook, but their hearts were united in their resolve. They were not just friends; they were a family bound by destiny and adventure, and together, they could face anything.